Seeing Solids and Silhouettes

3-D GEOMETRY

TERC

Investigations in Number, Data, and Space®

Dale Seymour Publications®

Menlo Park, California

The *Investigations* curriculum was developed at TERC (formerly Technical Education Research Centers) in collaboration with Kent State University and the State University of New York at Buffalo. The work was supported in part by National Science Foundation Grant No. ESI-9050210. TERC is a nonprofit company working to improve mathematics and science education. TERC is located at 2067 Massachusetts Avenue, Cambridge, MA 02140.

This project was supported, in part,
by the
National Science Foundation
Opinions expressed are those of the authors
and not necessarily those of the Foundation

Managing Editor: Catherine Anderson
Series Editor: Beverly Cory
Manuscript Editor: Karen Becker
ESL Consultant: Nancy Sokol Green
Production/Manufacturing Director: Janet Yearian
Production/Manufacturing Coordinator: Joe Conte
Design Manager: Jeff Kelly
Design: Don Taka
Illustrations: DJ Simison, Carl Yoshihara
Composition: Archetype Book Composition

This book is published by Dale Seymour Publications®, an imprint of Addison Wesley Longman, Inc.

Dale Seymour Publications
2725 Sand Hill Road
Menlo Park, CA 94025
Customer Service: 800-872-1100

Order number DS47003
ISBN 1-57232-756-1
16 17 18 19 20-ML- 07 06 05 04

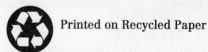

Printed on Recycled Paper

Contents

*Repeated-use sheet

*Repeated-use sheet

Make the Buildings

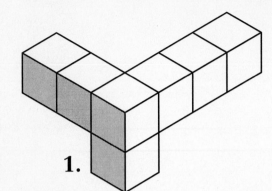

1.

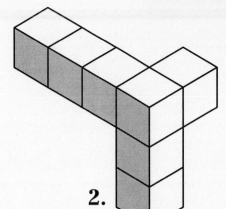

2.

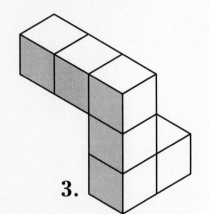

3.

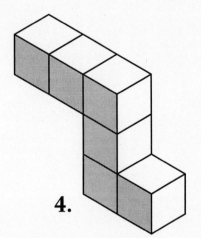

4.

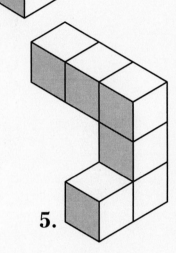

5.

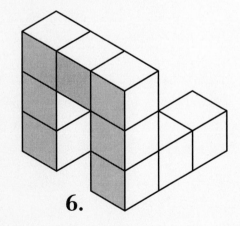

6.

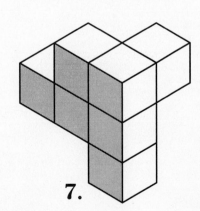

7.

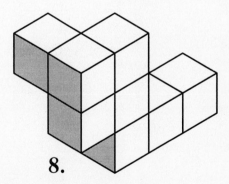

8.

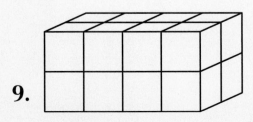

9.

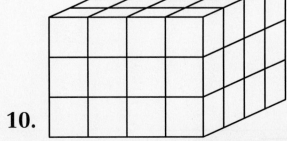

10.

1

Investigation 1 • Session 1
Seeing Solids and Silhouettes

How Many Cubes?

How many cubes does it take to make each building?
Predict. Then build with cubes to check.

1.

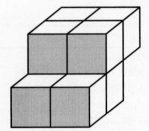

Prediction: _____ cubes

2.

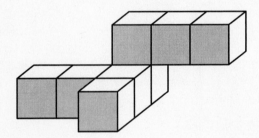

Prediction: _____ cubes

3.

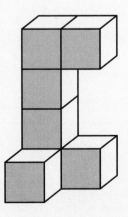

Prediction: _____ cubes

To the Family

How Many Cubes?

Session 1

Math Content
Interpreting 2-D drawings of 3-D structures made out of cubes

Materials
Student Sheet 2
Pencil

In class, we have been looking at drawings of buildings made out of interlocking cubes and then using cubes to try to make the buildings. For homework, your child will predict how many cubes are needed to make the three cube buildings shown in the pictures on Student Sheet 2. Tomorrow in class, students will have the opportunity to check the predictions by making the buildings with cubes. You might ask your child to describe his or her strategy for predicting the number of cubes and to explain why that guess is reasonable.

3-D Challenges

Challenge 1

How many unit cubes would it take to make this building?

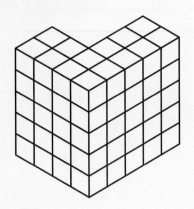

Challenge 2

Make this building with cubes. How many cubes did you use?

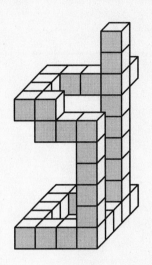

Challenge 3

Can you make a cube building like this?

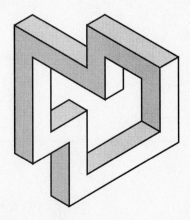

Silhouettes of Geometric Solids

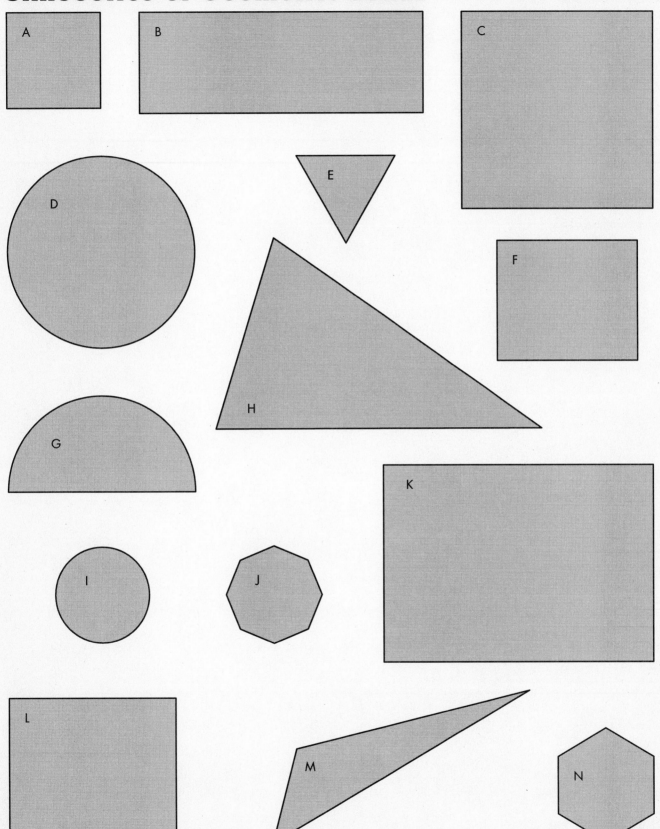

Investigation 2 • Sessions 1–2
Seeing Solids and Silhouettes

Landscape 1

Build this landscape with your geometric solids. Then look at each pair of silhouettes below. Find all the points in the landscape from which you could see both silhouettes in a pair. Write the letters of these points beside the silhouettes.

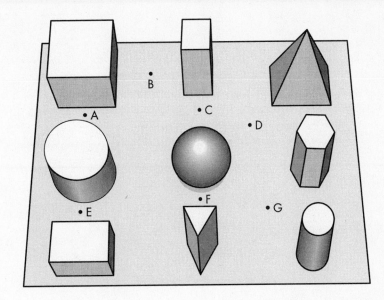

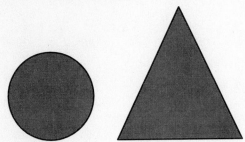

Pair 1

Points from which these could be seen:

_____

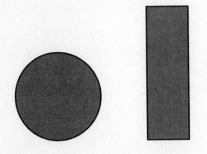

Pair 2

Points from which these could be seen:

_____

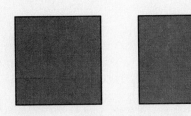

Pair 3

Points from which these could be seen:

_____

Landscape 2

Build this landscape with your geometric solids. Then look at each pair of silhouettes below. Find all the points in the landscape from which you could see both silhouettes in a pair. Write the letters of these points beside the silhouettes.

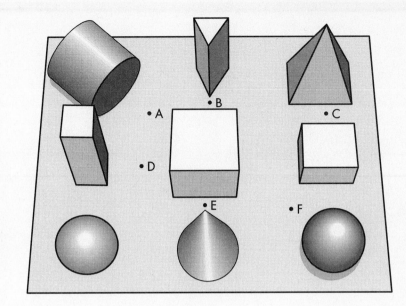

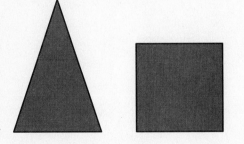

Pair 1

Points from which these could be seen:

_____

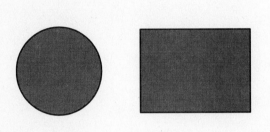

Pair 2

Points from which these could be seen:

_____

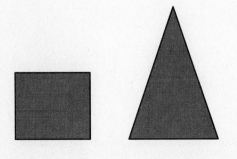

Pair 3

Points from which these could be seen:

_____

Landscape 3

Build this landscape with your geometric solids. Then look at each pair of silhouettes below. Find all the points in the landscape from which you could see both silhouettes in a pair. Write the letters of these points beside the silhouettes.

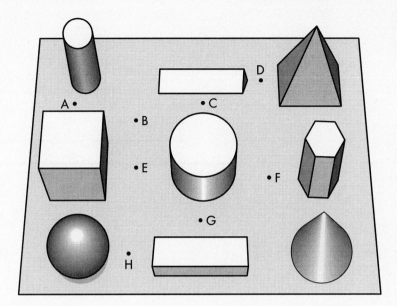

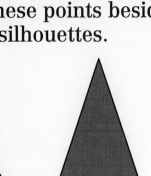

Pair 1

Points from which these could be seen:

_____

Pair 2

Points from which these could be seen:

_____

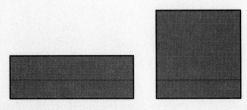

Pair 3

Points from which these could be seen:

_____

Landscapes Challenge

Look at this pair of silhouettes. Find all the points in the three geometric landscapes from which these two silhouettes could be seen. Write the letters of those points.

These could be seen from the following points:

In Landscape 1:

_____

In Landscape 2:

_____

In Landscape 3:

_____

Match the Silhouettes

An artist was walking around a museum.
Five giant geometric solids were on display.
The artist stopped here and there
to draw silhouettes of what she saw.

She drew one silhouette of each solid
from somewhere on the museum floor.

Match each silhouette to one of the geometric solids.

Geometric Solids

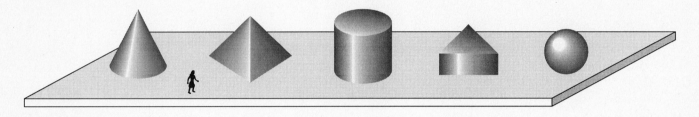

Letter: _____   _____   _____   _____   _____

Silhouettes

A   B   C   D   E

Drawing Silhouettes: An Introduction

Use cubes to make this building.

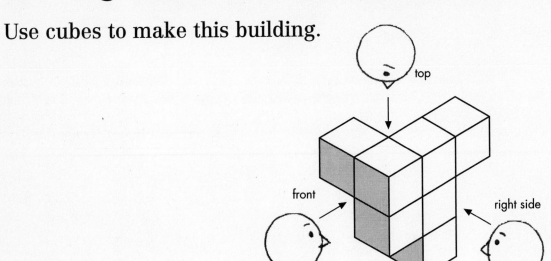

Two silhouettes of the building are shown below.
One was seen from the front, and one from the right side.
The silhouettes are drawn on graph paper so we can see
where the cubes are.

What do you think the top silhouette looks like?

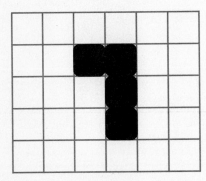

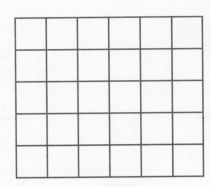

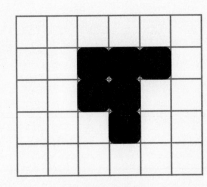

Front   Top   Right side

Front, Top, and Side Silhouettes

Make each building with cubes.
Then draw the silhouettes for both.

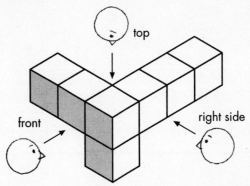

1.

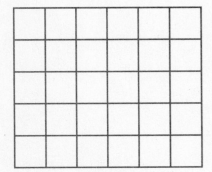   <table><tr><td> </td></tr></table>   <table></table>

Front	Top, as seen from the front	Right side

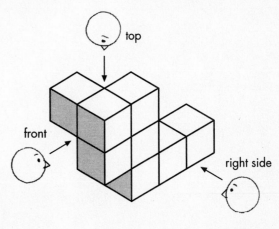

2.

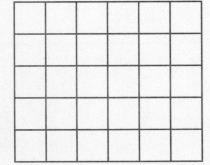

Front	Top, as seen from the front	Right side

Drawing Silhouettes A and B

A. Try to draw the three silhouettes for this building. Don't use cubes.

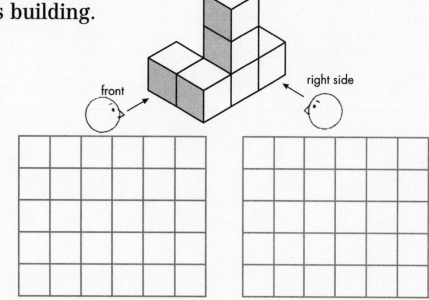

Front   Top, as seen from the front   Right side

B. Make the building with cubes. Then draw the three silhouettes.

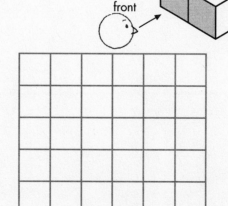
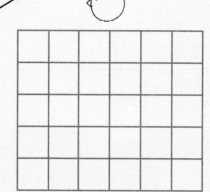

Front   Top, as seen from the front   Right side

Drawing Silhouettes C and D

C. Try to draw the three silhouettes for this building. Don't use cubes.

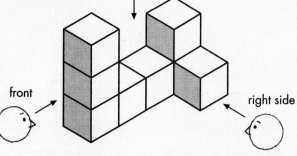

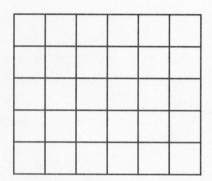 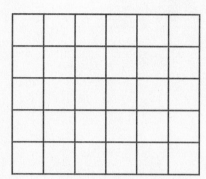 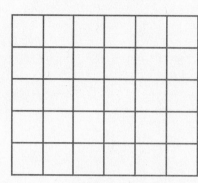

Front   Top, as seen from the front   Right side

D. Make the building with cubes. Then draw the three silhouettes.

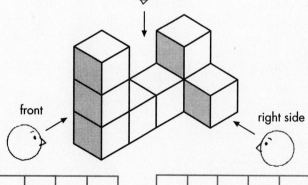

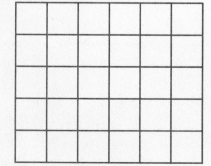  

Front   Top, as seen from the front   Right side

Puzzles: Building from Silhouettes

For each puzzle below, construct a cube building that makes the three silhouettes. Do any other buildings also make these silhouettes?

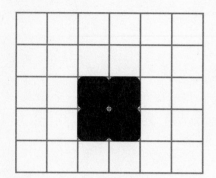   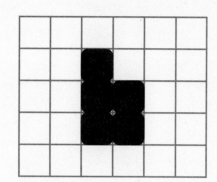   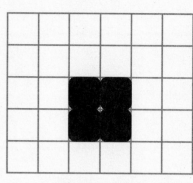

1.   Front   Top, as seen from the front   Right side

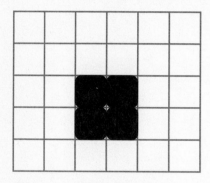   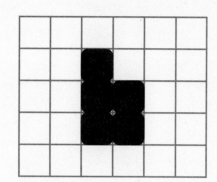   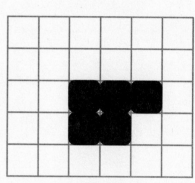

2.   Front   Top, as seen from the front   Right side

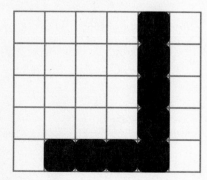   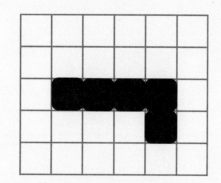   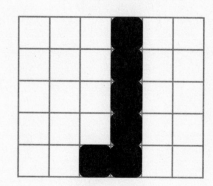

3.   Front   Top, as seen from the front   Right side

Challenge: How many different cube buildings make the three silhouettes in puzzle 1? in puzzles 2 and 3?

Cube Buildings

Draw the silhouettes of these three buildings
from the front, top, and right side.

1.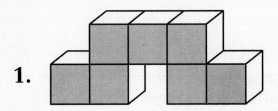

2.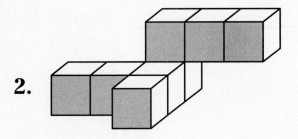

3.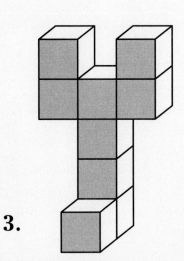

To the Family

Cube Buildings and Cube Silhouettes

Sessions 3–4

Math Content
Visualizing what objects look like from different perspectives

Materials
Student Sheet 15
Student Sheet 16
Pencil

In class, students were given a picture of a cube building and then drew the top, front, and right-side silhouettes. Then we worked in the reverse: given the top, front, and right-side silhouettes, students constructed the matching cube buildings. For homework, your child will use Student Sheet 16 to record drawings of the front, top, and right-side view silhouettes for each of the three buildings shown on Student Sheet 15. Encourage your child to explain the strategy she or he uses to imagine how the building would look from each view and what shadow it would cast. If your child expresses confusion about how to think about the top view, remind her or him to draw the top as viewed from the front.

Cube Silhouettes

Draw the front, top, and side silhouettes for three cube buildings. Put the number of the building above its silhouettes.

Building number _____

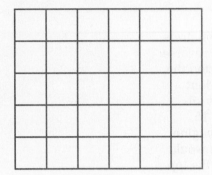   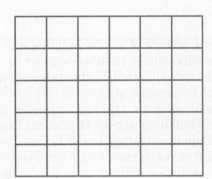   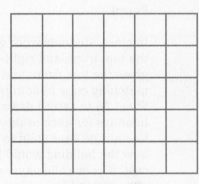

Front   Top, as seen from the front   Right side

Building number _____

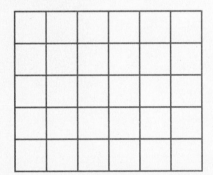   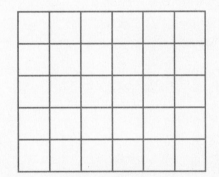   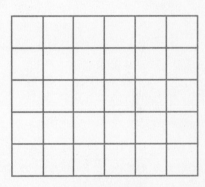

Front   Top, as seen from the front   Right side

Building number _____

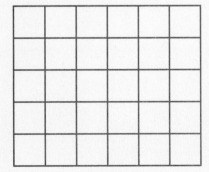   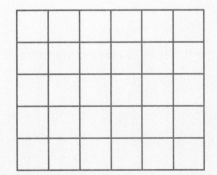   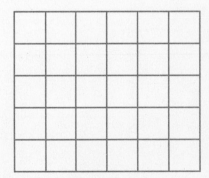

Front   Top, as seen from the front   Right side

To the Family

Cube Buildings and Cube Silhouettes

Sessions 3–4

Math Content
Visualizing what objects look like from different perspectives

Materials
Student Sheet 15
Student Sheet 16
Pencil

In class, students were given a picture of a cube building and then drew the top, front, and right-side silhouettes. Then we worked in the reverse: given the top, front, and right-side silhouettes, students constructed the matching cube buildings. For homework, your child will use Student Sheet 16 to record drawings of the front, top, and right-side view silhouettes for each of the three buildings shown on Student Sheet 15. Encourage your child to explain the strategy she or he uses to imagine how the building would look from each view and what shadow it would cast. If your child expresses confusion about how to think about the top view, remind her or him to draw the top as viewed from the front.

Mystery Silhouettes

List objects you find at home that make silhouettes
that are these shapes. The size of the silhouette
doesn't have to match.

1.  Object(s) I found that make a square
silhouette:

_____

_____

2.  Object(s) I found that make a triangular
silhouette:

_____

_____

3.  Object(s) I found that make both a rectan-
gular silhouette and a circular silhouette:

_____

_____

On a separate sheet of paper or on the back of this
sheet, draw a silhouette of an object you find at home.
The class will try to guess the object you chose from
the silhouette you draw.

To the Family

Mystery Silhouettes

Sessions 3–4

Math Content
Understanding how 3-D solids project shadows with 2-D shapes

Materials
Student Sheet 17
Household objects with simple geometric shapes
Pencil

In class, students have been investigating the different shapes of silhouettes made by projecting cube buildings positioned in different ways on the overhead projector. For homework, your child will look for objects at home that make the silhouettes shown on Student Sheet 17. On the back of the sheet or on a separate piece of paper, your child will then draw a silhouette of some object he or she finds at home; tomorrow, the class will try to guess what the object is, on the basis of the mystery silhouette. Encourage your child to think about how the shadows projected by the object will depend on how he or she holds it to a light. If your child is having difficulty imagining the shadows an object would cast, you may want to suggest using a bright light aimed at a blank wall in a darkened room.

Different Views of a City

This map shows the top view of a cube city.

The eight buildings shown are made from interlocking cubes.

The number on each building tells how many cubes high that building is.

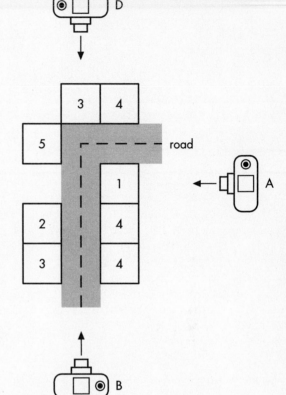

A photographer flew around the city in a helicopter and took four silhouette photographs.

The photographs were taken from points A, B, C, and D (looking in the directions of the arrows).

The resulting silhouettes are shown here. Below each one, write the letter of the point where it was taken.

1. ___   2. ___   3. ___   4. ___

37

More Cube Buildings

Draw the silhouettes of these three buildings from the front, top, and right side.

1.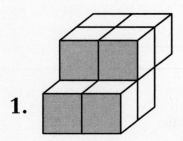

2.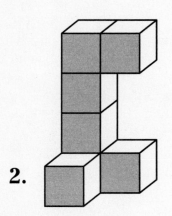

3.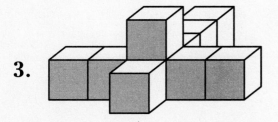

To the Family

More Cube Buildings and Cube Silhouettes

Session 1

Math Content
Visualizing what objects look like from different perspectives

Materials
Student Sheet 19
Student Sheet 16
Pencil

In class, we have been writing instructions that tell others how to put together a simple cube building and then evaluating those instructions on the basis of how well other students can use them to recreate their buildings. For homework tonight, your child will draw silhouettes of the buildings shown on Student Sheet 19 from three different views (top, front, and right-side). Your child will record the silhouettes on Student Sheet 16.

Cube Silhouettes

Draw the front, top, and side silhouettes for three cube buildings.
Put the number of the building above its silhouettes.

Building number _____

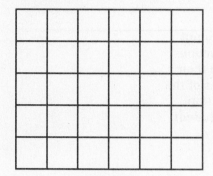

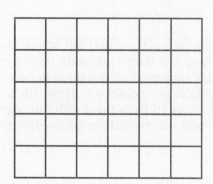

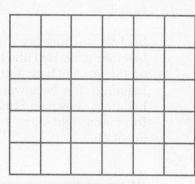

Front   Top, as seen from the front   Right side

Building number _____

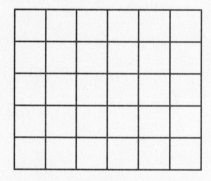

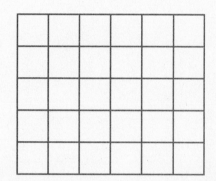

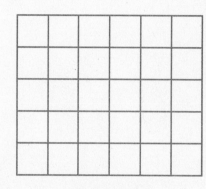

Front   Top, as seen from the front   Right side

Building number _____

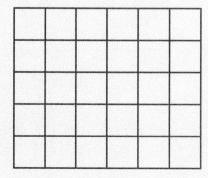

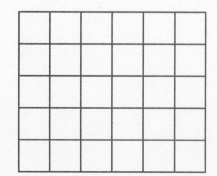

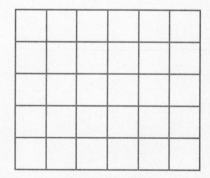

Front   Top, as seen from the front   Right side

To the Family

More Cube Buildings and Cube Silhouettes

Session 1

Math Content
Visualizing what objects look like from different perspectives

Materials
Student Sheet 19
Student Sheet 16
Pencil

In class, we have been writing instructions that tell others how to put together a simple cube building and then evaluating those instructions on the basis of how well other students can use them to recreate their buildings. For homework tonight, your child will draw silhouettes of the buildings shown on Student Sheet 19 from three different views (top, front, and right-side). Your child will record the silhouettes on Student Sheet 16.

Building Instructions Set A:
3-D Picture

Make a building out of ten cubes by looking at its picture below.

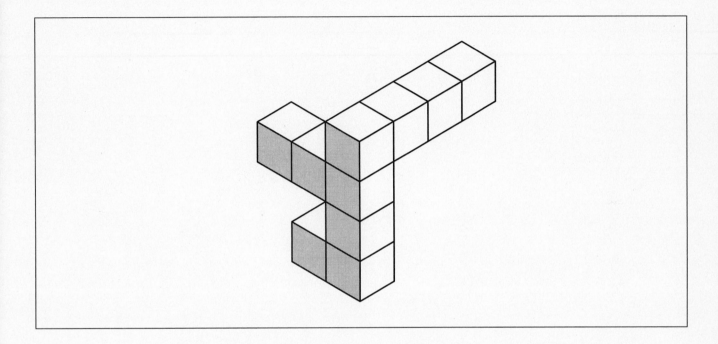

Are these good instructions for making a cube building?

_____

_____

Tell what is good and what is bad about these instructions.

_____

_____

_____

_____

_____

Building Instructions Set B:
Three Straight-On Views

Make a building out of ten cubes by looking at the three pictures of it below.

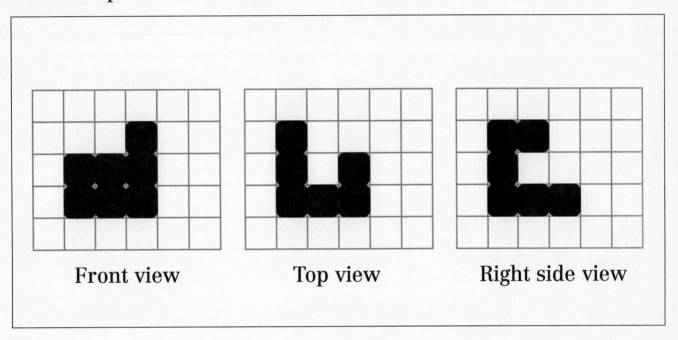

Front view   Top view   Right side view

Are these good instructions for making a cube building?

_____

_____

Tell what is good and what is bad about these instructions.

_____

_____

_____

_____

_____

Building Instructions Set C:
Two Straight-On Views

Make a building out of ten cubes by looking at
the two pictures of it below.

Are these good instructions for making a cube building?

_____

_____

Tell what is good and what is bad about these instructions.

_____

_____

_____

_____

_____

Building Instructions Set D:
Layer-by-Layer Plans

Make a building out of ten cubes by looking at the plans below.

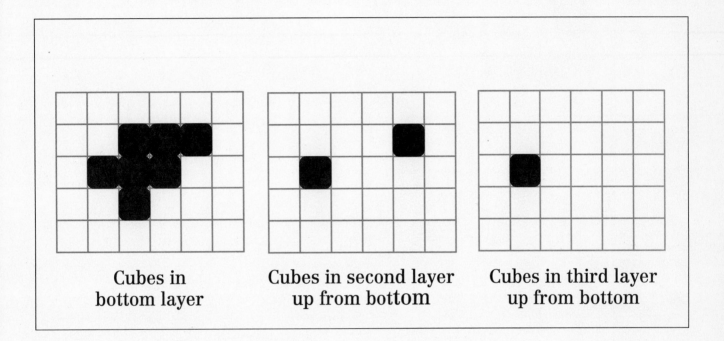

| Cubes in bottom layer | Cubes in second layer up from bottom | Cubes in third layer up from bottom |

Are these good instructions for making a cube building?

_____

_____

Tell what is good and what is bad about these instructions.

_____

_____

_____

_____

_____

_____

Building Instructions Set E: Written Directions

Make a building out of ten cubes by reading the written directions below.

> Take five cubes and attach them to make a straight line. Take another three cubes and attach them to make a straight line. Lay both lines flat on a table, with both horizontal. Place the shorter line of cubes behind the longer line so that the shorter is placed evenly between the ends of the longer. Attach these two lines together.
>
> Now connect the two remaining cubes. Hold these two cubes so that they are sticking up from the table—they should be vertical. Now attach these two cubes to the top of the last cube on the right of the shorter line of cubes.

Are these good instructions for making a cube building?

_____

_____

Tell what is good and what is bad about these instructions.

_____

_____

_____

_____

_____

_____

Quick Image Geometric Designs

1. Cut out the Quick Images below.

2. The chooser picks a shape and turns it face up for 3 seconds.

3. The person drawing tries to draw the shape that was flashed from the image in his or her mind.

4. Repeat Steps 1 and 2 with the same shape so that the person drawing can revise.

5. Reveal the shape and compare it to the drawing. How did you see the image on successive flashes? How did you remember what the shape looked like?

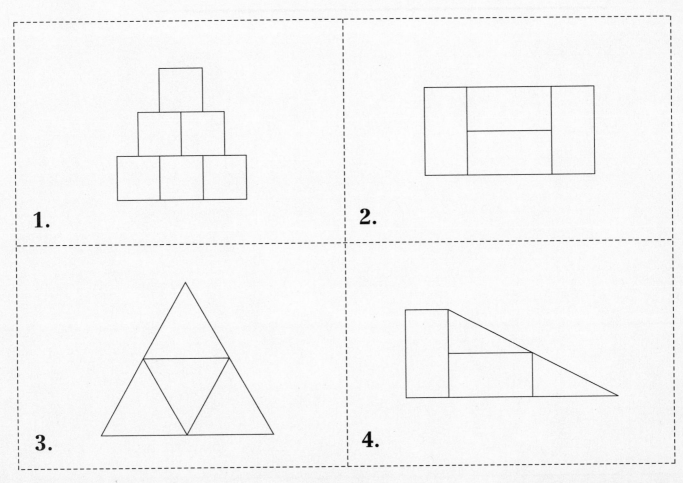

1.

2.

3.

4.

To the Family

Quick Image Geometric Designs

Sessions 2–3

Math Content
Developing visualization skills

Materials
Student Sheet 25
Scissors
Paper
Pencil

In class, we have been thinking about different kinds of instructions (3-D pictures, three- and two-view diagrams, layer-by-layer plans, and written directions) for building cube structures.

We have also been periodically spending ten or so minutes on an activity called Quick Images, in which students try to draw a design of geometric shapes that was flashed on the overhead for three seconds and then covered.

For homework, your child will play Quick Images with someone at home using the geometric designs (and directions) on Student Sheet 25.

ONE-CENTIMETER GRAPH PAPER

© Dale Seymour Publications®

57

ONE-CENTIMETER GRAPH PAPER

ONE-CENTIMETER GRAPH PAPER

63

ONE-CENTIMETER GRAPH PAPER

ONE-CENTIMETER GRAPH PAPER

ONE-CENTIMETER GRAPH PAPER

THREE-QUARTER-INCH GRAPH PAPER

Unit Resource
Seeing Solids and Silhouettes

77

THREE-QUARTER-INCH GRAPH PAPER

THREE-QUARTER-INCH GRAPH PAPER

87

Quick Image Dot Patterns

1. Cut out the Quick Images below.

2. The chooser picks a shape and turns it face up for 3 seconds.

3. The person drawing tries to draw the shape from the image in his or her mind.

4. Repeat Steps 1 and 2 with the same shape so that the person drawing can revise.

5. Reveal the shape and compare it to the drawing. How did you see the image on successive flashes? How did you remember what the shape looked like?

1.

2.

3.

4.

To the Family

Quick Image Dot Patterns

Sessions 1–4

Math Content
Developing visualization skills

Materials
Student Sheet 26
Scissors
Blank Paper
Pencil

In class, we have been continuing to write and evaluate instructions for making structures out of interlocking cubes. We've also been continuing our Quick Images work, this time with arrangements of dots. For homework, your child will play Quick Images with someone at home, using the dot patterns (and directions) on Student Sheet 26.

Make a Quick Image

On a sheet of graph paper, color 20 black squares in
an arrangement to use for Quick Images. Use the grid-
lines to help line up your squares in an arrangement
you think the class will remember. Try out your Quick
Image with a family member to see how difficult it is
for another person to remember and copy.

To the Family

Make a Quick Image

Sessions 1–4

Math Content
Developing visualization skills

Materials
Student Sheet 26 (for reference)
Student Sheet 27
Two sheets of graph paper (one to take back to school, one for practice)
Pencil (or black marker or pen)

In class, we have been continuing to write and evaluate instructions
for making structures out of interlocking cubes and to work with Quick
Images of dot patterns. For homework, your child will use graph paper
to make a dot pattern with 20 dots for classmates to copy during a
Quick Images activity at school. The directions are on Student Sheet 27.
Encourage your child to keep the pattern reasonable—challenging, but
not overwhelming. If it is too complex, other students will only become
frustrated. Your child may want to refer to Student Sheet 26 as a guide.

Quick Image Dot Patterns

1. Cut out the Quick Images below.

2. The chooser picks a shape and turns it face up for 3 seconds.

3. The person drawing tries to draw the shape from the image in his or her mind.

4. Repeat Steps 1 and 2 with the same shape so that the person drawing can revise.

5. Reveal the shape and compare it to the drawing. How did you see the image on successive flashes? How did you remember what the shape looked like?

1.

2.

3.

4.

ONE-CENTIMETER GRAPH PAPER

THREE-QUARTER-INCH GRAPH PAPER

© Dale Seymour Publications®

Unit Resource
Seeing Solids and Silhouettes

How to Play Close to 100

Materials
- One deck of Numeral Cards
- Close to 100 Score Sheet for each player

Players: 1, 2, or 3

How to Play

1. Deal out six Numeral Cards to each player.
2. Use any four of your cards to make two numbers. For example, a 6 and a 5 could make either 56 or 65. Wild Cards can be used as any numeral. Try to make numbers that, when added, give you a total that is close to 100.
3. Write these two numbers and their total on the Close to 100 Score Sheet. For example: $42 + 56 = 98$.
4. Find your score. Your score is the difference between your total and 100. For example, if your total is 98, your score is 2. If your total is 105, your score is 5.
5. Put the cards you used in a discard pile. Keep the two cards you didn't use for the next round.
6. For the next round, deal four new cards to each player. Make more numbers that come close to 100. When you run out of cards, mix up the discard pile and use them again.
7. Five rounds make one game. Total your scores for the five rounds. LOWEST score wins!

Scoring Variation

Write the score with plus and minus signs to show the direction of your total away from 100. For example: If your total is 98, your score is –2. If your total is 105, your score is +5. The total of these two scores would be +3. Your goal is to get a total score for five rounds that is close to 0.

Close to 100 Score Sheet

Name _____

Game 1   Score

Round 1: ___ ___ + ___ ___ = _____   _____

Round 2: ___ ___ + ___ ___ = _____   _____

Round 3: ___ ___ + ___ ___ = _____   _____

Round 4: ___ ___ + ___ ___ = _____   _____

Round 5: ___ ___ + ___ ___ = _____   _____

TOTAL SCORE _____

Name _____

Game 2   Score

Round 1: ___ ___ + ___ ___ = _____   _____

Round 2: ___ ___ + ___ ___ = _____   _____

Round 3: ___ ___ + ___ ___ = _____   _____

Round 4: ___ ___ + ___ ___ = _____   _____

Round 5: ___ ___ + ___ ___ = _____   _____

TOTAL SCORE _____

Close to 100 Score Sheet

Name _____

Game 1   Score

Round 1: ___ ___ + ___ ___ = _____   _____

Round 2: ___ ___ + ___ ___ = _____   _____

Round 3: ___ ___ + ___ ___ = _____   _____

Round 4: ___ ___ + ___ ___ = _____   _____

Round 5: ___ ___ + ___ ___ = _____   _____

TOTAL SCORE _____

Name _____

Game 2   Score

Round 1: ___ ___ + ___ ___ = _____   _____

Round 2: ___ ___ + ___ ___ = _____   _____

Round 3: ___ ___ + ___ ___ = _____   _____

Round 4: ___ ___ + ___ ___ = _____   _____

Round 5: ___ ___ + ___ ___ = _____   _____

TOTAL SCORE _____

Close to 100 Score Sheet

Name _____

Game 1   Score

Round 1: ___ ___ + ___ ___ = _____   _____

Round 2: ___ ___ + ___ ___ = _____   _____

Round 3: ___ ___ + ___ ___ = _____   _____

Round 4: ___ ___ + ___ ___ = _____   _____

Round 5: ___ ___ + ___ ___ = _____   _____

TOTAL SCORE _____

Name _____

Game 2   Score

Round 1: ___ ___ + ___ ___ = _____   _____

Round 2: ___ ___ + ___ ___ = _____   _____

Round 3: ___ ___ + ___ ___ = _____   _____

Round 4: ___ ___ + ___ ___ = _____   _____

Round 5: ___ ___ + ___ ___ = _____   _____

TOTAL SCORE _____

Seeing Solids and Silhouettes

Close to 100 Score Sheet

Name _____

Game 1   Score

Round 1: ___ ___ + ___ ___ = _____   _____

Round 2: ___ ___ + ___ ___ = _____   _____

Round 3: ___ ___ + ___ ___ = _____   _____

Round 4: ___ ___ + ___ ___ = _____   _____

Round 5: ___ ___ + ___ ___ = _____   _____

TOTAL SCORE _____

Name _____

Game 2   Score

Round 1: ___ ___ + ___ ___ = _____   _____

Round 2: ___ ___ + ___ ___ = _____   _____

Round 3: ___ ___ + ___ ___ = _____   _____

Round 4: ___ ___ + ___ ___ = _____   _____

Round 5: ___ ___ + ___ ___ = _____   _____

TOTAL SCORE _____

115

0	0	1	1
0	0	1	1
2	2	3	3
2	2	3	3

4	4	5	5
4	4	5	5
<u>6</u>	<u>6</u>	7	7
<u>6</u>	<u>6</u>	7	7

8	8	<u>9</u>	<u>9</u>
8	8	<u>9</u>	<u>9</u>
WILD CARD	**WILD CARD**		
WILD CARD	**WILD CARD**		

Practice Page A

Find the total amount of money in two different ways.

> 1 half dollar
> 9 nickels
> 6 pennies
> 4 dimes

Here is the first way I found the total amount of money:

Here is the second way I found the total amount of money:

Practice Page B

Find the total amount of money in two different
ways.

>   4 quarters
>   8 pennies
>   9 nickels
>   2 dimes

Here is the first way I found the total amount
of money:

Here is the second way I found the total amount
of money:

 Name ___ Date ___

Practice Page C

Find the total amount of money in two different ways.

 1 half dollar
 5 quarters
 4 dimes
 3 nickels

Here is the first way I found the total amount of money:

Here is the second way I found the total amount of money:

Practice Page D

For each problem, show how you found your solution.

1. Five people want to share 32 pencils equally. How many pencils does each person get?

2. I have 32 pencils. I want to put them in boxes that hold 5 pencils each. How many boxes will I need?

3. I bought 5 boxes of pencils. I spent 32 dollars. How much did I spend on each box of pencils?

Practice Page E

For each problem, show how you found your solution.

1. Pablo uses color folders to organize his papers.
   He has 13 folders in each of four different colors.
   How many folders does he have altogether?

2. There are four books in a new science fiction series.
   In our class, 13 students each own the whole series
   of books. How many books do they own altogether?

3. Stephanie bought four "baker's dozen" rolls.
   A baker's dozen is 13 rolls. How many rolls
   did Stephanie buy?

Practice Page F

For each problem, show how you found your solution.

1. Twenty-eight gymnasts are going on a tour. They will perform together and individually. Each gymnast wants two minutes alone. How much "together time" will they have if their entire show is ninety minutes long?

2. The gymnasts get very thirsty during their performances. How many bottles of water are needed if they each drink three bottles during the show?

3. The gymnasts use ninety towels during each performance. How many towels does each of the twenty-eight gymnasts use?